DEAD RECKONING

Ron Overton

Acknowledgment is made to the editors of the following magazines
in which some of these poems first appeared:
Apple, Cape Rock Journal, Commonweal, Epos, Nassau Review, New,
The New Salt Creek Reader, Rapport, Soundings (Stony Brook),
Street Magazine, Sumac, Tamarack, Tentacle, Windless Orchard
and Wisconsin Review.

The author wishes to thank the National Endowment for the Arts
for a Writing Fellowship which aided in the completion of this book.

Library of Congress
Catalog Card No.: 79-67058

ISBN: 0-935252-11-8

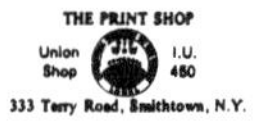

STREET PRESS
Box 555
Port Jefferson, New York
11777

for friends

CONTENTS

An Early Memory

Smoke still dribbles from the engine.
Its black clockwork shifts & clanks.
Steam seeps everywhere. The train
reclines against the bank
like someone who can't go on.

Deep inside, I hear a dog exhale
a muted human cry.
We have not allowed for this.
A crane tapped the trestle,
throwing everything off.
In the red light
a woman wanders in her slippers
among firemen,
her bold shadow cast back on the wreck,
walking toward the crowd,
toward us —
my appalled mother, my grave father
holding me in his thick
unyielding arms

Uncle Moss

Old Moss,
lean and silent,
two rattling sticks for eyes —
never knowing paper rustle,
branches snap — wild surmise
upon his brow.

He'd venture out along the street,
stroll in the garden a minute or two,
long enough to raise the sparrows —
then fix himself in his dusty flume
and circle the house
all afternoon.

Old Moss
left yesterday,
walked right out of his skin —
tapping on the fence posts,
raising the lean death rattle,
the summer wind humming.

The grass will grow back in.

The Tract

Flashlighting
to the Festival grounds,
jazz lacing the moonless night,
his grocery-boy face appears:
Here, take one of these.

The cheap print
runs in the drizzle
like the fear cupped in his immaculate eyes.
A fine night for a second birth.

But ahead, discarded, they
cover the wet path like scattered leaves.
So I pocket mine & jig a step or two
for a peony, a lost summer noon —
while a door quietly shuts in the skull,
wind lifts bright grass,
the hymnals close.

Miss Conklin

She sat among the tarnished 4 o'clock slants
of light, shivering like a high-strung
hummingbird dangling flower high (not from
chills or fever, but the wild dance
of shattered ganglia), grinning
from her roost above The Saturday Evening
Post. To stop the kittens from growing,
she winked, feed 'em on whiskey. In the beginning
she took the household by surprise; but soon
her Paisley presence was just another shade
among the shadows of the living room.
Her quiet vibration stopped today.
Dot's dead — not passed away, or lost. She's dead.
She's not gone home, or in this ink. She's dead.

1968

There's a strangeness
on things that pulls everything
to it — the limousines' crawl,
the candle's unsteady flame,
so much talk of men becoming vegetables.
We somehow manage to kill our best,

the TV complains.
Outside,
the pavement shines with a June rain.
Six months ago plows worked here, all night,
in the empty, white streets,
shaping and reshaping the darkness.

The cat watched, held to his sill —
his quick, restless body full of snow.
I can still see
his darting nose and tensed feet.
And the fact of his getting there —
impossible, before the leap.

Spring now, he's outside sniffing under
some random bush.
Office girls in bright reds appear
like robins
and carefully pick their way thru the rain
to their Mustangs.

They're off for the Cape.

December Aubade
for Linda

Half awake, I pull and drift in
    the light, plush weaving
of your neat laughter, your uncertain
    eyes, words deliciously breaking
between your lips; these tease the brim
    of this too sudden, early waking.

Slowly I stumble back, to the dancing
    and song of my dream,
but it is gone, like a moment
    of white winter breath —
the brush of you against
    this too cold morning.

Moon Shot

Both sit outside in patio chairs,
lolling in the funhouse heat.
These are the bickering pinball sons
of the balding sergeant downstairs
who watch the sprinkler's languid arms
and mumble curses at the dog.

The older one is teaching the younger
how to smoke a cigarette.
Waiting for the lunar bulletins,
they exhale luxuriously
and dream of guns with bores the size
of a starlet's bust.

Their limbs are long, bony, listless.
They are asleep on the seas of the moon.

Photographs

May I speak this
    clearly to you who
taking me over
    so quietly have

to change the room
    created an empty
space. I was slow
    to understand that

love is difficult
    unless you're bored
and random — **nothing**
    is **plumb, level**

or square, except
    perhaps the saying
of it. So that you
    can understand this

fear, these pictures
    will not do — I
should wash the stiff-
    ness from love, rub

its public face with
    dirt, and will — so
that we see our-
    selves, not standing

like this, in ease
    and clarity, but
deeper, deep be-
    neath the surface

of these images,
    a grim breathing
of small birds, their
    throbbing bones, yet

strong, hungry as
    the jerking eye
of the black snake
    waiting below.

A Confusion

You instruct me in silence.
There is a light snow falling
in your eyes, or

the slow turning of the sea.
I can't tell which.

Belgium, by Train

1

The neat patched hills
are stashed with summer grain,
all groomed for show; cottages,
red barns, long military rows of trees
flick by, casual curve
of sheep's shank & neck,
goat's nod, white
against the morning's
underwater green —

2

So,
around me,
big women primp & fuss
for such a day,
Dandy Conductor rubs his rump
against a pole, adjusts his cap
& neatly grins.

Details pat.
Train's on time.

3

Later, Bruges:
six plump daughters of prosperous loins,
of sunshine & lace,
& an old salt with stumped hand.
They bob & chirp
about his grizzled head or,
in trices of silence,
starched collars white
as cake, glance
toward the rushing pane, touch
they know their soft
brown hair —

4

Then lulled,
the light dissolves:
heavy clack of steel,
sweet odor of coastal air —

swaying toward cities
whose cobbled streets we begin to walk,
even now,
nodding to sleep.

Tangier Ferry

Thoughtless gulls depend, puppeting
above blue glacial wake,
slip back, then belly up, spill
into the orange sky, receding
deeper and deeper, swallowed
in the yawn of African dark.

Later, in the bar
I meander on their blank oceans:
they have become abstraction —
only their black-marble eyes
remain, and the silent dream
of their endless turning
against the last red flames
of the sun.

The Compartment

1

Next to the window
an old con, Meknes born.
His wrist is like a 2 x 4.

He downs everything with love —
black sardines, hard-cheese, bread,
red wine, wet green pears.

After dinner,
from his wooden suitcase:
anise whiskey we dare not refuse.

2

A 6 foot 6 bald priest,
his proud habit girded with thick rope.
He smiles, holds sacramentally

a lit cigarette
plumb to the swaying floor. The trick topples,
he nods with pleasure, leaning

to the train's motion.
A companion, a novitiate, hands like birds
nestled in his lap.

3

Later, all asleep —
an aimless guitar
in the next compartment,

a boy's voice from California.
He's lost his girl, a car accident.
He doesn't believe in God, or home.

At dawn
we creak past waking San Sebastian.
Sun-spokes, headache, the guitar again.

Cincinnati

I read two poets and
they both sing Cincinnati!
The first was gladly born there,
the second returns in spring to Cincinnati
to recall a tramp on a concrete bench
and Saint Rose of Lima's timid chimes.
I'd read the city strange to me,
had built it of unspecific brick & stack,
but remember it now — suddenly —
for a rush-hour sally downtown for VW parts,
for the vegetable calm of Kentucky
beyond the sullen gold river
of our retreat.

In celebration,
I decide to dream of recovered Cincinnati —
of its drumming Stuart Davis factories,
its plush green borders,
its centipede name. . .
But my dream is the Midtown Tunnel
traffic logy eyes a sudden glaze of snow
a sideways skid past the tollbooth
my hands won't unfist
in the knotted dark
my feet
won't reach the brake

Long Island

A photograph, teasing —
forked limbs, black crotch
heaped with wet Michigan snow,

snow covering the cairn,
the rise beyond, the footpath —
on the wrist snow, in the weeds,

& somewhere out of the picture,
whole counties of ice where nothing stirs
but winter dusk: all

measure for this heat, island damp
blunting mind, bones, flesh:
only this ache

for snow, for cold, for dark.

The Walks

Love, like a stone,
a magical stone
I won't lift, for
the shining of

it that I can
never speak about, for
fear of what's be-
neath — pale worms,

what? — I've
come to you with
the nervous eyes of a
cat, have kept a mad-

man's lidded pulse
all night — for you.
We've entered strange
theaters, our shadows

have crossed the
screen, the crowd
hoots — So we've gone down
narrow streets, oh,

walking our dog, Despair,
you nodding your what
the doctor mistakes for
red hair, me awake

with no singing. What
words we both look for
and never find — yet
then are pleased, later,

uncoiled in a moment's
room — released,
as dusk covers
the red city.

Childhood

Like the boozed duet two rooms down
in the Eight Pines Motel that
almost comes clear,
memory almost has the summer day I
was feeling good &
pulled the brake & rolled
the old imperious Hupmobile into the street
my sister brought up today.
But no: not quite.
The song of getting yelled at,
maybe.
A slap's flashbulb white.
A tantrum, on the rose-cluttered rug.
But not the fat deed, not the clear riding:

that star behind the wheel,
that wasn't me

Anatomy of the Crow
for Dale Parish

1

Crow
is an October bird.
His Jolson routine goes best

against a Molotov cocktailed sky.
And he knows it.
While other birds stentorially sail

and adjust their collars
like J. Edgar Hoover,
he shuffles

and mugs.
He doesn't glide.
His decline is a trick —

he hitches
his pants up
very quick.

He caws
and affects all over the sky.
Doubletalk is what he flies.

2

Alias —
Blackbird. Raven. Rook.
Innocents! Don't judge him

by his counselor look.
In his eyes you'll find
fool's gold

and soot.
His coat was filched
from the back of the moon.

His legs are gilded sticks.
He stays up all night
and sleeps till noon.

And each evening the knave
sings a ribald song
on a gentleman's grave.

3

He has
his good points though.
He is concise,

is tough against the weather,
withholds advice,
and though disorderly

can fly like hell
when the wind is right.
His anarchy

is venial.
His deceit sneaks
toward pure delight.

He's autumn's quip
upon itself,
a quickened Yorick

brought back
for one last gag
before the kingdom falls,

a black joke
in the wind's solemnity,
a poem clenched in the teeth.

He knows
his act depends
on holocaust, and so,

like the frantic blazing leaves,
he revels loudest
at the end.

Seeing an X-Ray of My Knee

bothers me.
This peels a part of me
I've never seen:
this is new.
Stark conspiracy
of bone & bone.
Bare fact.

Far worse than dreams
of bus terminals
without your pants.
Somewhere, you've left behind
your modest skin.
You've gone all the way.
X-rays are what nudists
hide under the bed.

No grin here,
no witty signature.
Nothing worth a silver frame.
Just the ghostly map,
white on black.
Your most secret self,
plot for your novel, fleshy life:
standard as the doctor's
textbook chart.

Pinup
of chalky bone.
Of what we leave,
when we leave.
Of what the democratic worm gets
down to, in the end,
underground.

My blanched remains.

The Airplane

1

From a middle distance,
the slim blue body juts out
of the ground like a broken leg.
Or it looks like a blue toy
flung down in a child's pique.
Or a shark that's tumbled from the sky
on its face.
Take your pick.

Closer, the floppy head
trapped inside the cockpit
which they are casually jimmying open
looks like the floppy head
of a dead man.

2

As you may have guessed,
this is all a lie.
I pulled a muscle playing tennis
and pretend it happened in a plane crash.
I am not the dead pilot of course
I am the only survivor.

Trial

Samuel Kwolinski
(standing in his overalls),
didst thou not,
with malice and intent,
crush the shapeless life
of thy three-month son,
when in a fit of rage
didst throw at him a pumpkin?

Aye, dead he be,
though not by my intent —
'twas done, my lord,
by the hand of fate
that did strike mine,
and turning the ill-thrown ball
from a course
directed at my wife
to the carriage of my son,
crushed his three months into none.

What is spoken may be true,
but thine office to thy wife
is not to hurtle vegetable.

Fruit, my lord —
a pumpkin is a fruit.

Femme Fatale

She is whispered about,
praised above other belles
but not actually seen till Act II.
Enters late, as usual,
bearing a willful red parasol.
There shall be a duel.

You immediately love her.

She strolls in the city,
a heart-shaped scaffold collapses on Jim.
She attends the Queen's Regatta,
the yachts mysteriously veer & collide.
She weds a magician,
his hands turn to stone.
In '29 she charms the Stock Exchange.
She breaks the Hindenburg's heart.

You must have her.

A Separation

Like all of us,
notes he once could reach
are lost, not there.
The tarnished trumpet sputters
in the empty dawn.
I hesitate upon the stair.

Thru the pale window;
dishes strewn in the sink,
the Grade-B movie moving
across the wall,
the unmade bed.

He's living spare.
He calls it holy.

After Borges

you are convinced
you are locked inside yourself:
eyes no more than plate glass,
your soul like a pit,
hard & central.

The gold cat ambles in, curious,
& collapses on the warm carpet.

Saplings by the hundreds
lurch in the wind, outside.
Behind them, the pale
unglittering bronze of the sun.
Cold spring light.
Flesh smells of
earth, water, rust. . . .

Though the sun slips away
you are convinced time, etc.,
are illusions.

Your heart thumps once,
days may have passed.

Opening to the Contortionist

It is always happening.
I look up CHIASMUS,
or DEVELOPMENT, for the spelling.
And there she is,
poised on a straightback chair,
her head planted between her 2 ballet slippers,
ankles in her ears,
looking discreetly amused.

Her taut lips say:
skip the sideshow compassion,
this is as it should be.
Look,
Hands below, holding on,
knees on top, arched in a perfect M,
head squarely in the middle,
at the true center
of everything.
My revisions are just.

I can't agree.

True,
I don't think she feels pain,
only hard pleasure,
at putting things so.
But her smile seems the smile too
of strain almost held back.
I don't know.
Perhaps it's just pride.
I have gone where no body goes,
I have complicated myself
beyond all understanding.

Whatever her point is,
she has made it.
She makes me uncomfortable.
My knotted Mona Lisa.
I turn her page,
wandering toward the word I want,
her smile mysteriously hung
in the midair of my life.
I feel limited,
lost,
in my stiff cage of bone.

Teaching Whitman

I see Walter Whitman
laughing at me —
in my Pringle sweater,
my Hanover loafers,
my socks Stretchable,
my Rooster tie —
all shined & brushed,
scrubbed & blocked.

I manage small promises to him,
who bawls, "There's a wise old man
in you!," who ransacks the earth
shoving his nose in every dark space.

And you — you are dumb, in your chairs,
to the edge of killing.

For a Former Student, Killed Instantly

All I can see are the sudden
white eyes of death, the crystal bright
assault, the body's lunge
and catch,
an explosion of ice.
But that's enough.

There always seemed more death in Daley's
stockyard paunch or Hershey's claw
than in a Ford sedan. My innocence.

So you've rubbed my nose
in mortality — now you instruct,
and force this treaty
against that blinding light.

Why the Grades Aren't In

The lately usual,
4 AM, cat hair on the keys
can't get through the papers

(O, I sometimes love their bones
but not all the time their prose) —
I drink from

my bright yellow cup
(psychotic, they say) tin cup
& bright yellow daffodils

of the table,
thinking, this is crazy
all these responsibilities

& what I hear
is a poem yawning about fish
that tilt to the light

& yellow, yellow
of taxis warblers hydrants
pencils & lemons.

The Cigar
for Mike Lopes

I finally smoked it.
It's been an amulet in my briefcase
for more than a year, cohabitating
with bitchy notes, books,

papers I can't bring myself to grade,
clips, pens & sandwiches.
God knows, it's been through hell —
not just the stodgy company, but

dropped from the hip each Friday,
gone half a continent on useless chores,
& worst, run over by the Volvo
after a particularly bad day last fall.

Yet it's endured, its taste is rich,
it's a pleasure to smoke.
Peace & health to your good son David
who walks now & marvels at fish.

Autumn News

The walnuts have dropped
to blacken & sulk
in the stiff October grass;
the thorns are falling asleep.
Bright bees are reported
sacking the last of the grapes today.
The maple's leaves
have abandoned their calm colors,
they're beginning to riot
in yellow & red.
They are expected to fall.
And the kingly white sun
has gone down in a different way,
leaving a zone of cold
around the house.
Night, and a breeze
cleans your eyes awake:
the silver circus of stars
performs overhead! Today,
the news is old.

Carnivore
for John Ratti

When my gaze
blossoms
on his devouring brain,
he stops, looks up.
He holds my presence in his slack,
bestial eye.
Waiting for my human move.
His catch,
the squirrel's small, severed head,
glistens grail-like
in the moon's cool light.
He's caught between this caution
& necessity.
Then,
like the old wish to hurt
to rip & devour
buried deep in even a gentleman's heart,
he stirs
& slips far back
into the dark.

The Millet Moth

1

One by one they fold
prayerfully against the wall,
white as brides: first five,
then ten, then twenty —
their gathering goes beyond counting!
What a congress of white!
Regatta becalmed
in the trough of night.

2

One flutters on my ankle,
I carefully lift him off:
white dust on my flesh.
Again I'm turned as in dream
to the stone-dead seas of the moon,
to the planets' abysmal steppes,
where his bruised, flickering wing
would be bright amulet.

Bermudas

My new, inland wife
sleeps well beside me, strolling
in pastel gardens of coral, flower & fish.
She will not see the old burnt hulk
touched by the moon, urged softly
from its emerald cove,
from the land,
out to the ancient reefs.
This shard of time is lost to her —
she will not see the relic masts,
the skewed slant of beam & spike that ride
the sea tonight.

Alone, sleepless, I watch:
none of the lolled crew cares for salvation —
they pass a cigarette from hand
to hand, slipping further out, laughing
and exchanging tales like children,
keeping no watch,
eight feet above the tangled history
of the sea.

Ceremony
for Jeff & Sue

Thanks for the New Year.
Sorry we never made the word games,
the numb came subtly, suddenly,
dredging our Helen Trent histories up
(Bad Art, Bad Art, you nod & laugh) —
10 o'clock, 11, minutes, then
sure as time or the fall of proud kings,
the gay ball slithering down
Ben's slick hysteria.

Later, in the kitchen,
stuffed clams, champagne; a stand-
up comic somewhere in the house drones on
about the Pope. We pause and hang
without resolve, like sleeping fish.

There's a dense snow outside now, falling,
moving graceful and even in the night.
It's an old ceremony we are half aware of
tickling softly on the pane, filling
the yard's thickets, limning
the dark roots of the new year.
When it started is anybody's guess.

Partial Eclipse

The yard rests in sudden clarity —
the roller leans eternally against the shed,
the neat stack of salvaged wood
has always been there streaked with light
like this, the feeder with the lampshade to keep the cats
from climbing up — every object stained,
at poise in antique light.

We squint through strips of negatives —
old girl friends, tulips, class trips to the zoo —
to watch the disc erode;
but our eyes fall back to the still, green world
and love, alive in our faces like scurrying birds,
these move our hands more than the sudden chill —
at poise in this new world.

Cat in the Rain
Mulligan 1966-77

Through the window,
the only yellow.

Curled in my eye
asleep, despite

the loamy afternoon.
Or yesterday, on

the patchwork quilt
in blue milky

light. Late
spring. Awake.

Least Terns

They weigh
as much as thought
and are white,
describing prim circles
on a sky so dazzling blue
your eyes ache —

and when they fall,
they drop
like the suicide
and rip
the mottled green skin
of the sea
for their prey

Grasshopper Leg

The upper half is sun
bleached, ivory of old piano keys
and sea shells, tapers
smoothly as

a schoolgirl's calf
to marble knee.
Lower half, more wizened, sea-
green counterpart, dark

glassy twig
with twin row of minute thorn,
curved as the edge
of glass blade. The

hinge is perfect,
still works! This is a find,
my fingers sense it —
silence after song, yet

earnest of love, promise
kept by the earth — something to pocket,
in a meadow of billboard
and glaring steel.

Musicians

Listen to this.
I took a thick green tongue
of grass, strung it tight
between my thumbs
and played the blues.

Such lean, dark song
the tortoise-shell cat
(who has been hurt in many dark ways)
stood martial still — two soft tears
sweetly spilled from the gold bowls
in her antique eyes.

We played the juice
right out of that green thing,
went sullen all afternoon.

For Ann, *Felidae*

Having sprung from
a nest in the wilderness
of the backyard
& transient loins I

suppose your interest
in civilization is
as slight as the whisker
of your guilt — Oh

you'll hum for
us sure toy with July
if we tear it from
the year & palm it to

a ball for you.
And you'll strut
brood preen even wink
all the civil things

for a square meal.
But you're wild Ann
sleek engine of felinity
compact of coils

feints crouches jabs
you polish seriously —
we keep you not
we know for the cross

on your back the Dumbo
ears the punchy circles
you spin in but
for your disdain for

what's possible —
the improper jungle you
are stolen from & always
stealthing toward.

Monadnock
for Ken Clauser

1 The Base

We all exult
we could have stayed up there (alone!)
for days. And mean it too.
But walking back along the bleached log-road
Thoreau shrugs his shoulder & leaves:
no cool austerity of granite or birch
for the climber back on the ground,
no green season turning on its axis of ice,
but GO-GO GIRLS — 3 of them! — big hot blondes
dancing, leaping naked in the woods for me!
flecks of sunlight on their ample asses,
the eager, peach-colored flesh
in the trees like fire

2 The Descent

Going down the sheer, southern slope
turns easy — a cadence takes the feet,
they swing out recklessly, flutter with fatigue,
then find the foothold (rock, earth, root)
the rhythm prepares: poet choosing
the words he keeps.

3 **The Tree Line**

The third poem
isn't done yet. Give me time.
It's about the climbing point right
on the tree line where the trees turn
skeletal & grey, like driftwood, then stop.
It begins: **From here on it's all rock
and extravagant sky —**
And about the joy climbing above the tree line,
taking lordly steps up the blocks of stone,
the body gymnast-light in the blue air,
breaking through! The tissue moon —

Give me time.
I want to get things right.

After Mingus

we go to Macy's &
in the dead light of fluorescence

& dusk we
snap at each other.

The manikins smile.
They have spread their picnic cloth.

You gliding downward to Perfumes
like Eurydice,

me lost in a crowd
of coats, faces

drowning in glass.
That soft tolling,

no song
to call us back.

The Watch

What time is it?
I've forgotten my watch at your house
and so must drive on these back roads alone,
without even its dull heart
for company.
It is time to go slower.
Muskrats and squirrels and cats
lie heaped in the headlights.
From a thicket, two eyes burn:
then go dark.
And when someone behaves without restraint,
we say
he behaves like an animal.

Dead Reckoning

Ignoring the stars,
I watch a new toad tack from lawn
to cinder to bush,
heading out —
improvising
a course toward a muted light
he remembers
along his spine.
And, somewhere, keeping track.

Compass.
Log.
I have come this far.
Who can say he is lost
for sure?

Waking to the News

Olson or whoever it was was right:
we're governed by the worst.
And the worst mouth off.

Even before the sun is up
we suffer under their language.
Their words slip from the radio

to bury in the brain's pink.
Later, just when we're beginning to feel good,
they hatch. That's it,

they've got another day.
On the Evening News a mouth opens,
closes like a valve.

We think we are free of it.
In a dream that night the words
wash ashore like oil.

Lights

The rain has finally stopped.
A spaniel wind scratches at the window.

From here the town's lights
are lyric, song taken through the bone —
a few tall red points in a row,
many more glacial points of white
over the tar pit of the town.

How like snow, yet
crazily they burn, breath
of some unfocused star
glistening on the dark cloth in my mind —

scattered glass of a broken moon,
song heard only once,
then carried off by the frugal wind.

Dead Reckoning

Published in a first edition of 500 hand-bound copies.
The first 50 are signed by the poet.

Printed on Howard 70 Lb. Lively Ivory Antique Laid text.
Cover is Navajo 65 Lb. Fieldstone Ivory.
Endpapers are Cortlea 80 Lb. Sunlight Yellow.

Printed on ATF Chief 22
at The Print Shop, Smithtown, N.Y.,
in September, 1979.

This is copy: